Summary

of

Ordinary Grace
William Kent Krueger

Conversation Starters

By BookHabits

Tips for Using BookHabits Conversation Starters:

EVERY GOOD BOOK CONTAINS A WORLD FAR DEEPER THAN the surface of its pages. The characters and their world come alive through the words on the pages, yet the characters and its world still live on. Questions herein are designed to bring us beneath the surface of the page and invite us into the world that lives on. These questions can be used to:

- Foster a deeper understanding of the book
- Promote an atmosphere of discussion for groups
- Assist in the study of the book, either individually or corporately
- Explore unseen realms of the book as never seen before

About Us:

THROUGH YEARS OF EXPERIENCE AND FIELD EXPERTISE, from newspaper featured book clubs to local library chapters, *BookHabits* can bring your book discussion to life. Host your book party as we discuss some of today's most widely read books.

Table of Contents

Introducing *Ordinary Grace*

FRANK DRUM LIVES WITH HIS BROTHER JAKE, HIS SISTER Ariel, and his parents in the town of New Bremen in Minnesota. His father is the priest of the local church, and his mother is in charge of the musical activities related to the church and the community. The summer of 1961 started with the death of Bobby Cole, a thirteen-year-old child. Very soon, it was followed by four more deaths. *Ordinary Grace* is about the summer of 1961, the deaths in New Bremen, the Drum family, and the grace of God in which believers have complete faith.

Frank is upset by the death of Bobby because it was the first time he had encountered death. The incident bothered him more because Bobby was Frank's age and made him think about death. Soon after, Frank comes across another body; a dead man found lying near the railway tracks. Rifling through his pockets was a Dakota man called Redstone. Frank and Jake keep his secret and don't give him away to the men who later come to investigate. A few days later, Ariel is found dead and floating in the river near the tracks.

Ariel's death deeply affects the family, and questions of faith and love rise among the remaining four members. While Frank and his father hold on steadfastly to their faith in God, and even lean on it for support, Jake and his mother want nothing to do with faith any longer because they feel let down. Ariel was the most talented of the siblings and was studying music with Emil Brandt, an old time lover of her mother and a renowned musician in his own right. He was blind and lived with his sister, who had a major mental illness and was deaf. Ariel was also going steady with Karl Brandt, a nephew of Emil.

Redmond was claimed to be implicated in the murder mainly because he was a Native American and a local policeman, Doyle, was a racist psychopath. As the summer went on, the drama unraveled, showing cracks in the family and the community. Frank ultimately learns to forgive, but not before two more deaths have taken place. *Ordinary Grace* also explores the themes of racism, the effects of war on men, the role of a pastor, the grace of God, and the different ways in which people deal with loss. There is also a thread of mental illness and social condemnation running throughout the plot. A book with a large scope, the ultimate question raised is whether those who believe in God can sustain their belief after a senseless loss like the untimely death of a loved one.

Discussion Questions

"Get Ready to Enter a New World"

Tip: Begin with questions dealing with broader issues to ensure ample time for quality discussions. Read through all discussion questions before engaging.

~~~

question 1

Born a Crime deals with issues surrounding the apartheid in South Africa.
What did you know about the apartheid before reading this book? What did
you learn about the apartheid from reading this book?

~~~

question 2

There are several stories about Trevor Noah's upbringing in *Born a Crime*.
Which of the stories was your favorite story to read?

~~~

question 3

Born a Crime is the story of Patricia, Trevor's mother, more than it is about Trevor. Why do you think he chose to write his story in this way?

~~~

question 4

Patricia was an enormous influence on her son, Trevor Noah. What do you think was the most important lesson Patricia taught Trevor?

~~~

question 5

It is evident that religion plays a large role in the life of Trevor Noah and his family in *Born a Crime*. Why do you think religion is so important to the family?

~~~

question 6

In *Born a Crime*, Trevor Noah compares Catholic school to the apartheid because they are both cruel and authoritarian. What evidence is there in the book to support this statement?

question 7

In South Africa at the time of Trevor Noah's birth, interracial relationships were illegal. Why do you think the government made it illegal?

question 8

Consider the response to Patricia's claims that her husband is abusing her.
How do the people in her life respond differently to this abuse?

question 9

When Patricia goes to the police to tell them she is being abused by her husband, they choose not to report it. Why do you think this is?

~~~

question 10

What was your initial impression to Trevor Noah and his mother, Patricia? How did your impression of them change after finishing *Born a Crime*?

~~~

question 11

Trevor learns lessons about love in *Born a Crime*. What are some of these lessons?

question 12

When Trevor Noah and his mother would walk together, she would often have to let go of his hand if the police would be nearby. It seems a bit cruel, but why do you think she did this?

~~~

~~~

question 13

Trevor Noah was alone, without other children to play with, for much of his childhood. How do you think this affected his development?

~~~

.

question 14

Trevor Noah describes himself as a chameleon as a child. How do you think this affected him?

~~~

~~~

question 15

Trevor Noah grew up with his father and later his stepfather in the house. How is his relationship with his father different than the relationship with his stepfather? How do you think his relationships with these male figures affected him?

~~~

~~~

question 16

One reader stated that Trevor Noah's voice comes through clearly through his words in *Born a Crime*. What are your thoughts on Noah's voice in the book?

~~~

~~~

question 17

Many readers walked away from *Born a Crime* with admiration and respect for Trevor Noah. How did you feel about Noah after reading this book?

~~~

question 18

Born a Crime became a number one bestseller for *The New York Times*. Why do you think this book became successful?

~~~

question 19

Parade called *Born a Crime* "unforgettable." What do you think it is about Trevor Noah's memoir that will stick with readers after they have finished reading?

~~~

~~~

question 20

USA Today referred to *Born a Crime* as a "gift" to Trevor Noah's mother and a gift to the readers. Why do you think this book is a gift?

~~~

Introducing the Author

BEST KNOWN FOR HIS CORK O'CONNOR SERIES OF MURDER mysteries, William Kent Krueger is a very popular writer with several awards under his belt, including winning the Anthony Award twice and the Edgar Award once. He also won the Barry Award, the Minnesota Book Award, and more.

William Kent Krueger was born in Torrington, Wyoming, but spent his childhood being shuttled from one place to another due to his family's impoverishment. When he grew up, he got a scholarship to attend Stanford University. After one year of a relatively peaceful life, Krueger took part in the demonstrations against the Vietnam War. He joined in a takeover of the President's office to protest against Stanford's complicity in weapons production. This put an end to his scholarship, forcing him to leave Stanford, leaving his education incomplete for the time being.

He moved to Nebraska to be with the woman he loved. He and his wife, Diane, moved to Minnesota so that Diane could attend law school. Though Krueger had wanted to write since he was in the third grade and one of his stories was praised by his parents and teacher, it was at this time in his life that Krueger began to seriously think about a writing career. He got up at the crack of dawn to write for a few hours before he had to go to work. He began to write short stories at first, which were published. He slowly graduated to writing full-time.

Krueger is deeply influenced in his writing by Ernest Hemingway, Harper Lee, John Steinbeck, Scott Fitzgerald, and James Farrell, as well as by Tony Hillerman and James Lee Burke.

Currently, he lives with his wife and their two children in St. Paul, Minnesota.

Fireside Questions

"What would you do?"

Tip: These questions can be a fun exercise as it spurs creativity among the readers by allowing alternate scene endings and "if this was you" questions.

question 21

Trevor Noah began his career as an actor and radio host, but left his jobs in order to focus on comedy. Why do you think he did this?

~~~

question 22

As a child, Trevor Noah grew up with strong Catholic religious beliefs. How important do you think religion is to him today?

~~~

~~~

question 23

On *The Daily Show*, Trevor Noah discusses current events in the United States. What unique perspective does he have to offer on this subject considering is background?

~~~

question 24

After doing comedy and television for many years, Trevor Noah released his first book, *Born a Crime*, in 2017. What do you think inspired him to write a book?

~~~

question 25

Trevor Noah has achieved great success in the United States. Why do you think he has become so successful?

~~~

question 26

Trevor Noah decided to move to the United States in 2011. How would his life be different if he did not move to the United States?

question 27

Living with his stepfather greatly affected Trevor Noah. If his mother never met his stepfather, how might his life be different?

question 28

Trevor Noah grew up in South Africa during the apartheid, which lasted until 1994. In which ways would his life be different if he had grown up during the same time period, but in the United States?

~~~

question 29

Trevor Noah was able to navigate life by learning to speak several languages. If he had not learned these languages, how do you think his life would change?

~~~

~~~

question 30

After Trevor Noah's mother was shot by her ex-husband, she encouraged
Noah not to be angry with his stepfather. If you were in a similar situation,
would you have handled it in the same way as his mother?

~~~

question 31

As a child, Trevor Noah and his family had to hide the fact that they were a family. Today, Noah describes this experience growing up as normal, though painfully so.

question 32

At a visit to Brown University, Trevor Noah was invited to speak to a group of people. During his speaking engagement, he made it clear to the audience that his mother was his biggest influence in life.

~~~

question 33

According to Trevor Noah, parents should help their children understand rules and laws, but they should also allow them to be able to challenge them. Growing up, his mother was strict with him, but she would tell him to challenge him if he thought she was wrong.

question 34

Trevor Noah had an argument with host of TheBlaze, Tomi Lahren, in 2017 after Lahren made remarks that Noah strongly disagreed with. He invited her to *The Daily Show* to see what she was like when she was not in her environment. He also wanted to give her the chance to challenge his beliefs and see if they could hold up when challenged.

~~~

question 35

Trevor Noah describes stand-up comedy as therapy for him. In addition, he also enjoys it because he feels he can share his message more easily through comedy.

question 36

Trevor Noah feels it is his duty to make the world in which he live a better place to live. He believes that everyone is able to do the same. To change the entire world on one's own would be impossible, according to Noah, but it is possible to make the world where you live better.

~~~

question 37

In preparation for his show, Trevor Noah spends over an hour reading as much current events as he can. When he is speaking on current events, he tries to talk about only what he knows.

question 38

Trevor Noah says that living in the United States feels "weirdly familiar" for him. When he compares South Africa and the United States, he can see several similarities. One of the similarities is that black people have been oppressed, yet the countries are both considered to be a "melting pot" of cultures.

Quiz Questions

"Ready to Announce the Winners?"

Tip: Create a leaderboard and track scores to see who gets the most correct answers. Winners required. Prizes optional.

quiz question 1

Born a Crime is the memoir of Trevor Noah's life. Noah grew up in
_____, in the 1990s, during the apartheid.

~~~

quiz question 2

Trevor Noah's mother was a black, Xhosa woman. His father is a
_____ man from Switzerland.

quiz question 3

Trevor Noah learned to speak many different languages in order to fit in with
several different people. He refers to himself as a _____
because of this.

quiz question 4

As a child, Trevor Noah often visited _____, where his grandmother lived. He recalls witnessing several periods of unrest while living there.

quiz question 5

True or False: Trevor Noah's mother gave him the name Trevor because it had no meaning. She wanted him to be free to become the person he was meant to be without his name predetermining his path in life.

quiz question 6

True or False: Trevor Noah grew up in a wealthy family. He credits his upbringing for helping him become successful.

~~~

quiz question 7

True or False: Trevor Noah's mother ensured that Noah attended church
every Sunday. He also attended a Catholic school.

quiz question 8

Trevor Noah was born in _____, in South Africa. At the time of his birth, the relationship between his mother and father was illegal.

~~~

quiz question 9

The first television show Trevor Noah appeared on was called Isidingo. His
first radio show was called _____.

~~~

~~~

quiz question 10

True or False: Trevor worked for the BBC on the shows *QI* and *8 Out of 10 Cats*.

~~~

quiz question 11

True or False: In 2014, Trevor Noah appeared on *The Daily Show*. The next year, it was announced that he would be John Stewart's successor as host for *The Daily Show*.

~~~

~~~

quiz question 12

True or False: The first book that Trevor Noah released was called *You Laugh But It's True*. It was published in 2012.

~~~

Quiz Answers

1. South Africa
2. White
3. Chameleon
4. Soweto
5. True
6. False
7. True
8. 1984
9. *Noah's Ark*
10. True
11. True
12. False

Ways to Continue Your Reading

EVERY month, our team runs through a wide selection of books to pick the best titles for readers and reading groups, and promotes these titles to our thousands of readers – sometimes with free downloads, sale dates, and additional brochures.

Want to register yourself or a book group? It's free and takes 1-click.

Register here.

On the Next Page…

Please write us your reviews! Any length would be fine but we'd appreciate hearing you more! We'd be SO grateful.

Till next time,

BookHabits

"Loving Books is Actually a Habit"

Made in the USA
Las Vegas, NV
08 December 2023

82344561R00037